We and She, You and Then, You Again

poems by

Leah Tieger

Finishing Line Press
Georgetown, Kentucky

We and She, You and Then, You Again

Copyright © 2017 by Leah Tieger
ISBN 978-1-63534-186-7 First Edition
All rights reserved under International and Pan-American Copyright Conventions.
No part of this book may be reproduced in any manner whatsoever without written permission from the publisher, except in the case of brief quotations embodied in critical articles and reviews.

ACKNOWLEDGMENTS

"Eat" first appeared in the Austin International Poetry Festival's 2016 anthology, *DI-VêRSé-CITY*.
"Galley Kitchen, Shotgun House" first appeared in the *Urge* anthology, Blue Thread Books, 2016.
"Three-Minute Affair" first appeared in *Thank You for Swallowing*, September, 2015.
A version of "I-30, I-20, Farm to Market Road" first appeared in *Redheaded Stepchild*, December, 2016.
"Eat" and "Only Her Name Returns" appeared in *The Dentonite*, January, 2017.

Publisher: Leah Maines

Editor: Christen Kincaid

Cover Art: Sara True

Author Photo: Steven McGann

Cover Design: Elizabeth Maines McCleavy

Printed in the USA on acid-free paper.
Order online: www.finishinglinepress.com
         also available on amazon.com

Author inquiries and mail orders:
Finishing Line Press
P. O. Box 1626
Georgetown, Kentucky 40324
U. S. A.

Table of Contents

We
Face/Sun 1
Cedar 2
Blanket 3
Like Nomads 4

She
And There Are Worlds Inside It 6
American Grandchild 7
Eat 8
Only Her Name Returns 9
Without Any Song 10

You
Fallow 12
Galley Kitchen, Shotgun House 13
Subtraction/Sextant 15
I-30, I-20, Farm to Market Road 16
Three-Minute Affair 18
Gulf 19

Then
A Headstone for Shafter 22

You Again
Planet Marfa 26

We

Face/Sun

In the beginning there were faces. On walls, sidewalks, clocks, benches and billboards. Most of them smile but some stare, grim and calm, at distant points on the horizon, at shifting destinations. Some look into their future, eyes wide, cheeks taut, unaware of what's coming and aware it's approaching all the same. Faces become maps, become compasses. Our feet face north, our pelvic bones twist to face our lovers, and our fingers turn to trace their abortive grasp. The sun burns our faces, scalds our eyes, grows wheat and we turn it into bread. It dries our clothes and bodies, keeps ice from forming most the time, keeps us from its encroachment, gauzy but cruel, inducing strokes, blindness, madness, and thirst, but not before we do it to ourselves and then each other first.

Cedar

Threads gather
where horizontal shadows fall

on our bed and bodies curving
into shapes that should be exclamation.

Moths float around the apartment
leaving us gray constellations

and we look for answers in punctuation.

Our questions
unwind us like sweaters.

We look through the holes in our clothing
and the room is shaped by ragged circles

so we ignore the corners, places
we hide the growing piles, small commas

made of dust and dried out wings.

Blanket

Clothes land like bodies without corpses
the rest of us left behind.
The rest of us searching reverse,
spools of film rewinding
because we want to get unwound again
with a slow whine,
that scream of machinery inside us
a breathing Rube Goldberg
built by proverbs of cloth and skin.
We read skin with fingers like we are paper.
Our illiterate hands try a fistful of hipbone and jaw.
We've never looked at someone else's ceiling so hard
or from so far away.
We've never looked at the insides
of another person's shoulder.
The comforter catches our blind faces
pushed into cloth
as if our lovers were blankets instead of people
and we've been wrapped in them since birth,
cradled by the only touch
that doesn't come from strangers.

Like Nomads

We lay out the damage like nomads
for sale on city blankets
old men on stoops with stories
of surgery and war.
We bare our wrists at each other
we bare our necks and navels
from skin that fails to register
until it's almost gone.
Lay out like cards a story
flashed out from camel trenches
from decks with endless prayers
this surgery is war.

She

And There Are Worlds Inside It

Her face a popped balloon.
A mouthful of sand.
The hum of machines inside a quiet room.

Her face rolled carpet, its chemical scent.
The mouth of a surfacing fish.

Her face a perennial bloom.
Its threat of return. An unbuilt fence.

Her face, the concrete poured and soft enough
to carve your name inside it.
A mailed letter. An envelope lost.

Her face caught like air
inside old glass.
An unturned faucet. A latch in the gate.

Her face a door, the hinges rusted.
It will not close or open.

A forest. The blade you use to cut it.
The lamp outside the door.

Her face torn pages.
Their soft and ragged edges.
A nest. A house
waiting to be lived in.

American Grandchild

She likes apartments over the garage,
keeps paintbrushes in her backpack,
eats umeboshi plums, and tells the story
of every run in her sheer black tights.
She's worn them under arctic light, the green
streaks, thick bands of pink in a dark sky.
She says she'll live somewhere European,
an American grandchild backward on Atlantic tide,
but she's seen the orbs in Marfa. She knows
their alien light inside her. She thinks of gravity
as a noose, her parents and lovers hangmen
threading the center. She chews her way out
and regrows her own limbs, becomes
a reminder, one dress in an empty closet.

Eat

Patient for flowers and being loved
she will stand in line and wait
quiet
when her lilies fall to the ground.
She watches you watching her
so she picks them up
and eats them
orders more
puts each color in her mouth
the melting stems collected there
a flood inside her,
mouth to mouth a rescue
of water from fountain.
Cold metal and chlorine
are bent over ceramic bowl
in her baptismal lapping.
Rounding the circle
where body folds into itself
she searches for center
drawing it out
plucking petals away from skin.
If she loves and loves you not
each repetition
will be closer to empty daisy,
nothing left but pistil until
she decides to swallow that too.
She devours the whole thing
even her fingers
and smiles at what's left of them.
She wipes her mouth
and tries to yawn. Instead,
she belches out a garden.

Only Her Name Returns

She fastens dropped blooms with pins and resin, with thread and tape. They fall on her floor faster than she can fix them. She lets them go, a whole carpet under her feet, a tiny hill, a mountain. Hikers pay her to guide them up its peak, to carry their luggage with a small pack of goats. Scientists come to study the trees. They come to study a new marsupial, name it and her mountain after themselves. Her house is covered in their bootprints. She tries to scrub them and then she lets them go, layer after layer, a new carpet to cover dead petals. Their soil yields fern and small grasses. Roses come and fall again. They grow mountains like jagged teeth and she climbs them all, furrows each canyon, finds a cave she can swim in. She searches until only her name returns, her name whispered by hikers, carved in the wood that was once her front door.

Without Any Song

This piece of her, of motor skills and memory,
moves like a flash of haunch in forest.
She'd love to compile the fragment somewhere,
make a museum, fill it with one lost sentence.
Outside of any proof of reincarnate life,
it would be kinder to go, to not build
anything inside her that sputters into being
and arrives already extinguished.
Staying is a pond. Staying is a body of water
that dips as if it's been ladled out of itself,
leaving a scar in the landscape until the cows
are almost starving. She watches them
as they stand in mute rows and bellow together
without any song. She knows she is like them
because they do not know why they are crying.

You

Fallow

You give all of it to her and forget
to keep any for anyone else.
You're sure she understands,
you steal it back,
and by it you mean your heart,
which she should know, because
what does any article detached
from object mean? And it,
the thing you gave her,
is a pulpy muscle, a perennial bulb.
It grows no matter where you plant it.
You bury it in soil, a lathed turning,
and wait for green to sprout there.
You forget to give it water.
You forget to put that patch of dirt
somewhere the sun can find it, and the sun
can't find its ass with its elbows,
blind as it is—
blind as everyone who stares too long—
and just as forgetful as you are.
What is it you're supposed to be growing?
Was it you or was it her?
Was it everyone? And what, exactly,
is a patch of dirt but a planet spinning,
roots dangling in its orbit, a kind of gravity,
both pulled and pulling, unearthed,
yanked out, and spinning from the surface.

Galley Kitchen, Shotgun House

You're inside it making cookies
for your niece's shower.

You're cracking all the eggs.

Their shells break like lace,
the carton unpeopled in tiny rows

too large to be mistaken
for the point of pen on paper,

the shape at the end of a sentence.

One yolk dries on the counter
and makes a small desert,

cracks into glaze on granite,
the stain so thin

you find it with your fingers
then scratch it away.

You lick the bowl
until there's nothing left

to clean with your body.

Flour covers the floor,
it follows you into your sheets,

and all you want

is to sleep inside the mess
as if you could warm it

into bread by morning, as if sleep
was a labor

and you could give birth.

Subtraction/Sextant

Scatter them on a dish.
Make the pieces part of yourself again
—all one hundred and fifteen pounds.

You're an atomic fraction of Earth, of six sextillion tons.

Walk the moon white
like an eye half-open in sleep
and your steps lose ninety-six pounds.

Space travel is not a valid diet.

Try floating. Your spine is a tongue
inside one quintillion, four hundred and fifty quadrillion
tons of watered salt.

Mariners don't weigh oceans. They weigh stars.

Scatter them on a dish.
Make men and meteors part of yourself again
—all one hundred and fourteen pounds.

I-30, I-20, Farm to Market Road

//

You wonder what lives are like in houses
surrounded by nothing but road and towers
filled with murder, so many eyes. You don't
remember birds in Watts staring from cement
and broken bottles like so many unsung Gaudis,
so many lonely men who made strange buildings
nobody's ever lived in. If only this road led to Spain
and oceans could be highways. You would see people
on either side and know all of them are drowning.

//

Stop to eat tortillas with butter, cooked the way
someone else's mother made them. Return
to your vehicle, pass trailers left in fields
like stubborn weeds. They'll grow west along the tracks,
trains a conveyance that's pulled and not propelled.
You want to go with them, build a home
in blue and orange boxes and find yourself on ships
in unknown countries, no place foreign enough
to forget you're still breathing identical air.

//

You turn at the wire frames of forgotten drive-ins,
pile old speakers in illegible glyphs, flecks of green
falling in the road, broken bottles under empty chairs
on an empty porch, their mismatched backs
an invitation, the postcard of someone else's view.
You leave your name in the mailbox and make
a new one, dream of where the old names went
on motel beds in bodies that almost look like you.

//

Shake rest stop napkins and loose change from your bag,
search for toothpaste and find nothing but yourself
in a scratched up mirror. Someone tried to take
the silver coating so you hold your thumb in front of you
and close one eye, paint your portrait on the tile wall.
The flat of your hand on your image cools the skin.
You catch your face in the mirror again and you're surprised
your eyes don't make you seasick from breathing.

//

You can't tell the difference between desert and ocean
without horizon, without the shifting line that forms
in your sight. You need to be seen like that. You need
an excuse to change into person, some reason
you can't come up with on your own, not in the fat middle
of nowhere with nothing but you undressing in silence
shadowed by the nodding of genuflect rigs.
You're going to climb their backs and ride them
like whales, burn your thighs on their metal skin.

Three-Minute Affair

*Good evening ladies,
you should join us for drinks.*

You should dance with us
so we can't talk

about your job and forget it
when the words leave your mouth.

You should dance with us
so we can't see your eyes

and ourselves
when we land in your gaze.

You should turn toward us
when we hold cigarettes

to let their small clip of fire
light your face.

And you should dance with us
around *carta blanca* tables

that remind us
of that diaspora feeling

which reminds us
of your face blown apart

into so many seeds.

Gulf

A wave's like sperm or poppies
a curved and collapsing thing

the pattern you saw on her shirt
when she walked the shore

soaking up oil on the driveway
while you mess with the car

as if such things were done anymore
on suburban Sundays

with lawn mowers and undershirts
grass and perspiration

expelled in cotton
flung from the body

in a pile on the floor.

There's crawdads in a bucket
on the flagstones in the yard

gawping mouths
small pieces of shit

red dumb bodies
in clear water

strange without stones
and other creatures

so you take them back to the shore
with your father

and decide
you will use them for bait

cast fractions
from their lost tomorrows

watch the tourists

hope there's a word
for subsequent minutes

the way there's a word
for subsequent days.

Then

A Headstone for Shafter

Then came
the falling price of silver

Then came
pockets of water in the tunnels

then
photographs and captions

Mine Superintendent, J.B. Little

His image covered
with glass panel and birdshit

Drill Operator, George E. Speed

That old Indian fighter
used diamonds to turn the ground

Company Physician, Peter Marshall
—brief selections taken from his prayers

I have no polished phrases
and Lord
often I have known failure

Cemetery, 1910

Each cross welded together
from old horseshoes

Mrs. Amparo Fuentes recalls her grandfather
buried there

His ore wagon pulled by sixteen mules
his rawhide whip

And her, sitting at the kitchen table
the flash still bright inside her glasses

pictures of small children
three generations
caught behind her on the fridge

You Again

Planet Marfa

Standup bass and banjo move like cartoons drawn by human hands.

Some pairs get close.

They sway under lights on wires, caught and hung like trophies.

The rest will find other arms. Hope is the space between songs.

It's not houses without roofs or windows.

It's not the sound guy complaining about his marriage.

You wish him better luck than you had.

                        Even if he's asking for something else

he just wants to know what it means to be a watered plant

with one more chance at breathing.

The band yodels its cry, a kind of waiting. Hope is the space between songs.

It's not bodies on the windshield when you drive away.

It's not pine and dry soil, tobacco, the cordite of falling stars.

Sound decays. Will you take it with you?

It is small enough to carry.

Thank You:

In no particular order and without words, because words are not enough:

April Bernard, Courtney Marie, Sara True, Bess Whitby, Sebastian Paramo, Vermont Studio Center, Rochelle Hurt, Marlin Jenkins, Josh Gaines, Emily Rose Kahn-Sheahan, Logen Cure, Bonnie Jo Stufflebeam, Fatima Hirsi, Lauren Belmore, every member of my family—nuclear and extended—and last, but never least, Steven McGann.

Leah Tieger lives in Dallas with her dog and her neighbor's errant chickens, and she resides in a small house with more windows than walls. She is a graduate of Bennington College—where she received an Academy of American Poets Prize—and she is working toward her master's degree at the University of North Texas. Tieger completed a residency at the Vermont Studio Center in 2016, and she wants to remain there like a stowaway on a transatlantic ship. Instead she helms a different boat, serving as cofounder and producer of the *Looped* poetry series, which has been hosted at the Nasher Sculpture Center and is sponsored by WordSpace, Dallas's largest literary nonprofit.

Tieger reads fiction for *The Boiler* and poetry for *The American Literary Review*, works as a freelance writer specializing in literature reference, and occasionally even writes her own poetry. Her poem "Galley Kitchen, Shotgun House" (which also appears in this chapbook) was a finalist for the 2016 Raynes Poetry Prize—judged by Alicia Ostriker. Her work appears in *Rattle, Gravel, Entropy, Voicemail Poems, Pretty Owl Poetry, Menacing Hedge,* and others. Like every good writer, the first draft of her first novel waits, quiet but restless, pushed to the back of proverbial drawer.

www.ingramcontent.com/pod-product-compliance
Lightning Source LLC
LaVergne TN
LVHW041514070426
835507LV00012B/1569